Disclaimer:

Every effort has been made to make our books and reports as accurate as possible. However, there may be mistakes, either typographical or in content. This content should be used as a general guide and not as the solution.

The author and publisher shall have neither liability nor responsibility to any person or entity with respect to any loss or damage alleged to be caused directly or indirectly by information provided in this report or book.

Introduction

Hello, everyone, and welcome to *WordPress Security*, the guide that'll teach you how to lock your WordPress site up so tight that even the most "1337" hackers won't be able to get into it. Not only will this perfect defense ensure your privacy and safety, it will give you peace of mind as well.

You may remember the brief security chapter I had in my previous guide, *WordPress Domination: Beginner to Ninja in 7 Days*.

`http://www.amazon.com/dp/B007LS0TLE`

This guide expands on that in a major way to show you a combination of beginner, intermediate, and advanced anti-hacking techniques, as well as a few other neat WordPress security tricks to keep your website protected.

The WordPress platform has become immensely popular for those who build websites online. This is due to an easy-to-use interface that requires no knowledge of complex coding, such as HTML or CSS, to use. WordPress also comes with some pretty heavy-duty security systems already in place. This is great for those who are new to website security and anti-hacking systems.

The problem lies in the fact that even the best security systems are vulnerable to crafty hackers who use the latest hacking and cracking techniques to get into your data. While the motivations of hackers and crackers can vary, 99% of the time, their intentions aren't good. Their intrusions can lead to serious consequences, like lost data, damaged coding and, in a worst-case scenario, identity theft.

The good news is that you can significantly beef up your WordPress site's inherent security with relative ease. You don't need to be a coding wizard to lock down your site and keep unwanted guests from accessing sensitive info or going on a code-destroying rampage within your system.

Most of the techniques I'm going to share are incredibly simple and can be done in a matter of minutes. Others may be a bit more advanced, but I'm going to walk you through the process and make sure that you have a good understanding of how to implement these security procedures so you can protect your site.

Now that you understand what this guide entails, let's get started and turn your WordPress site into an impenetrable Internet fortress!

Chapter 1: Hackers and Crackers: The Critical Difference

Every once in a while, you'll hear a news report about a hacker breaking into a system in a large company or causing some sort of trouble. Many people aren't aware, however, that the media incorrectly uses the term "hacker" when describing the situation.

Hackers are shown in television and movies as a sort of super-intelligent criminal. Sometimes they are fighting against a corrupt government or otherwise using their abilities for good. Other times, they are malicious and are terrorizing people with their skills. There are all sorts of fantasy hacker scenarios in entertainment, but when's the last time you saw a movie on someone labeled as a heroic or criminal *cracker*?

Reporters usually mix up the word "hacker" with the correct term, "cracker." Unless you enjoy computers or work closely with them, you probably don't know the difference.

In this guide, we will be using the term "hacker" to refer to someone that's breaking through your WordPress website's security. However, it is important that you understand the difference between the two phrases.

First, let's define what they mean. We'll start with the more popular expression, "hacker."

Hackers

A hacker is a person who is familiar with the internal systems of a computer or network. Hackers are enthusiastic about computers and enjoy exploring and learning about how they work. They are often computer programmers or designers.

The media often portrays the word in a criminal sense, and this is often where the non-technical crowd gets confused. When you hear on the news about a hacker attacking a bank, what they're actually referring to is a cracker.

It's important to realize that there is nothing illegal about being a hacker. The word doesn't imply that anything illicit is taking place. It is no more illegal to hack a system you own than it is for you to look under the hood of your car.

However, when someone else comes along and starts looking under your car's hood without your permission, then that is where the line gets crossed. There may also be laws regarding what kind of modifications you can make to your own car, such as installing tinted windows.

Hackers occasionally get in trouble by going too far. Once a hacker starts performing illegal actions through hacking, they can be correctly classified as a cracker.

Crackers

Crackers are also computer and network enthusiasts. The difference is that crackers use their knowledge of computer systems to break into secured systems that they have no authority over. Such actions include (but are not limited to) breaking into systems they do not have permission to access, stealing information, and corrupting data.

Even the legitimate use of the term "cracker" doesn't necessarily mean that something illegal is happening, though. Most crackers do their work illegally, but not all. Some companies hire crackers to intentionally break into their systems. This may sound crazy, but the goal is to expose weak spots that a real cracker could exploit so that they can be patched up.

Here, the cracker is legally doing an act that would normally be illegal. This is similar to how police may hire minors to attempt to buy alcohol at a bar, in an effort to test if the bar is following the law about checking the IDs of patrons.

If you really want to get your vocabulary correct, you'll have to throw some adjectives on there. Criminal crackers or malicious crackers are a few you could use.

You can think of crackers as being a type of hacker. Additionally, you could say crackers are hackers, but hackers aren't crackers. It's like saying all German Shepherds are dogs, but not all dogs are German Shepherds.

Why the Confusion?

Not a lot of people run around calling any dog they see a German Shepard. After all, a Golden Retriever and a Dalmatian are different breeds and wouldn't be classified as a German Shepard. So why have the words "cracker" and "hacker" become mixed up?

It may be in part that they sound so similar. They rhyme, and cracker has only one more letter than hacker. Additionally, their definitions are very similar.

Some hackers take offense to the use of the term. With the way the word is portrayed in movies and in the news, it leads people to believe that all hackers are crackers, and that being a hacker automatically means you commit crimes.

Remember, it isn't incorrect to refer to a cracker as a hacker, just as it wouldn't be wrong to call a German Shepard a dog. But when someone who isn't familiar with technological terms only hears the word "hacker" to describe these people, they have no reason not to believe that's the correct word.

With how the word "hacker" is used in the media, and has been for years, it can be acceptably used to refer to a cracker. Also, from this point forward, this guide refers to anyone attempting to break into your WordPress system as a hacker. However, it is important to know the difference between the two. This way, you can clarify if need be, and not make assumptions about people based on simply if you know they're a "hacker."

What Do Hackers Want?

What does a hacker stand to gain by breaking into your website? Some see it as a way to make a monetary gain. For example, a hacker who tries to steal credit card numbers from a bank may be trying to steal someone's bank account or identity. An identity can be sold and resold to a variety of buyers who would use it for illegal business practices.

Sometimes the hacker isn't after your money, however. Maybe you just happened to upset the wrong person, who then decides to have a vendetta against your website or blog. They may try to hack your site and take your server offline, disrupting business. They could also edit your website and put damaging information on your pages that would drive away readers or customers.

Perhaps a hacker stumbles onto your website. Suppose you've made a statement on your site that contradicts a strong belief the hacker holds. Instead of deciding to go on their merry way and agreeing to disagree, they may take this as a reason to attack you.

Also, there are hackers out there that simply love the idea of doing something naughty. These hackers tend to be in the younger generations, so they're looking to entertain themselves and prove how "cool" they are to their friends and strangers. They may not mean any serious harm to you, but the damage they can cause should still be taken seriously.

Hackers may look at your security system as a personal challenge, as if you're daring them to attack. Their pride compels them to try and take control of your system. There's no greater satisfaction for them than when they succeed—the more difficult the lock, the more interested they will be.

Whatever the case, it's important to keep your security tightly locked and updated. You never want to put your WordPress site at risk of being hacked. Following basic security precautions, keeping your system up-to-date, and having good security systems are vital to securing your website.

Chapter 2: Basic Steps to Stop a Hacker

Now that you have an idea of what the difference between a hacker and cracker is, and why they may try to get into your site, we can concentrate on preventing a security breach. Most of these techniques are very basic and easy to implement; others are a bit more advanced, though not hard. First, let's start by examining what you can do to prevent offline or in-network threats to your website.

Offline and In-Network Threat Prevention

Believe it or not, many people have their WordPress site's security compromised not by an online hacker, but rather by someone offline or within their network, such as a LAN or cloud-computing group. In fact, people tend to overlook this aspect of website security so often that this is one of the easiest ways for hackers to get into your system. All the online security in the world won't matter if your website isn't protected from real-life threats.

Shared Computers

This is one of the most common ways to have your website broken into. Many people share computers, either at work, at home, or in public places such as libraries and net cafes. When you access your website's admin area on a shared computer, you are putting yourself at risk. Due to this, it is advised that you don't access your admin area on *any* shared computers.

However, realistically there may be times when you have to do this. If you only have one computer in your home, then this may be unavoidable. But there are ways to compensate for this security risk.

The first and most basic rule is to not click the "Remember Me" box on the login screen. This will ensure that you, or a potential threat, will have to type in the login info manually each time.

When you're done working on your site on a shared computer, *always* log out. If you want to be extra safe, you can go into the computer's history and delete the cookies as well.

Never access your website's admin area on shared computers in libraries, hotels, net cafés or similar places. You have no idea how secure these computers are. A crafty hacker could have installed a key-logger program or some other exploit that can record your login information and get into your account. For this same reason, you should also avoid accessing your admin area from a friend's smart phone or tablet device.

File Transfer Protocol

FTP is one of the easiest ways to upload files to your WordPress site, but if you aren't careful, it could present a security risk. When you use FTP, not only are you gaining access to your WordPress site, but also every single file that is on your hosting server. If you have multiple sites, a hacker would only have to get into your FTP account to access them all. This could be disastrous.

Reducing the risk of an FTP-based intrusion is much the same as preventing other offline and in-network threats: limiting access. When you use your FTP client, make sure you create a password-protected profile for each website, as well as the root domain if it will let you. Different FTP programs will have different security measures, but most should have this basic function.

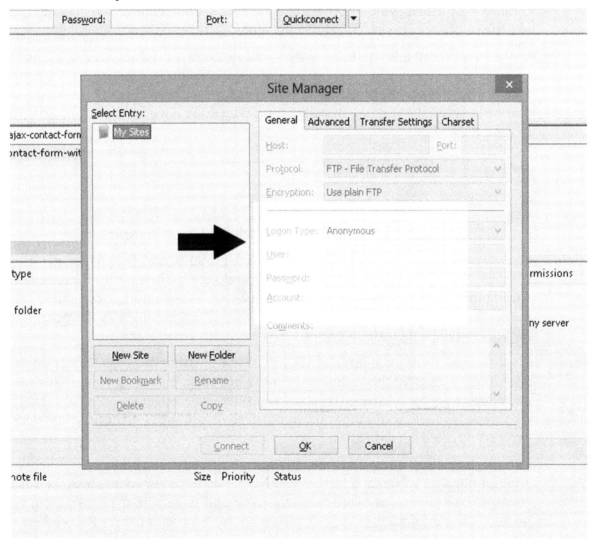

Also, while the quick-link can be a handy way to quickly access your files using an FTP program, you're going to want to avoid using this, especially on a shared computer. If for some reason you do use this function, make sure you delete the history once you're done transferring files.

Shared Servers

When you get a hosting account with a mainstream hosting company, like Host Gator or Bluehost, you will be on a shared server unless you pay for an expensive private server. This can represent a security risk in some cases.

While these companies do have exceptional security procedures and systems in place to protect you, you may want to get additional info on what you can do to lock down your server. This will be different for each web-hosting company, so you will likely have to email or call them if they don't have a section on security in their FAQ.

Network Vulnerabilities

Accessing your website's admin area while connected to a network can pose a huge security risk. This is even truer if you're using a LAN, as opposed to cloud computing or virtual private networks, which tend to be more secure.

The general idea behind a LAN or local work-group is that people can get into certain folders on each other's computers and access shared files. This can be very helpful, but it can also present a major risk. When another computer can access your files, even if it is an isolated "shared" folder, there is the potential for hacking since they already have a way into your computer.

Even worse, if one computer on the network gets hacked, the hacker could potentially access all the computers on the network, including yours. This can pave the way for viruses, Trojans, root-kits, key-loggers and other nasty surprises. If you're accessing your admin area or using FTP to access your web server, this could spell disaster.

The most obvious way to prevent this from happening is simply to not access your admin area while on a LAN. If you have no choice but to do so, make sure you speak with your network administrator and ensure that proper security protocols are in place for every single computer on the network. Remember, a chain is only as strong as its weakest link.

Generally speaking, cloud-computing networks and VPNs have top-notch security systems in place to prevent intrusion. Security protocols include Internet Protocol Security, Transport Layer Security, Datagram Transport Layer Security, Secure Shell (a great alternative to FTP), and more.

Username Issues

If your user name is obvious, it makes it much easier for a real-life threat to get into your admin account. Whatever you do, do not use "admin" as your username for your admin account. Once someone knows your username, it isn't hard for them to use brute force tactics to hack your password.

If you have named your admin username "admin," I would recommend making another admin account and deleting that one.

To create a new admin account, simply click the tab on the left-hand menu in the WordPress admin area that says "Users," then click where it says "Add New." Give the new account administrative privileges, log out, log into that new account, and then delete your old admin account.

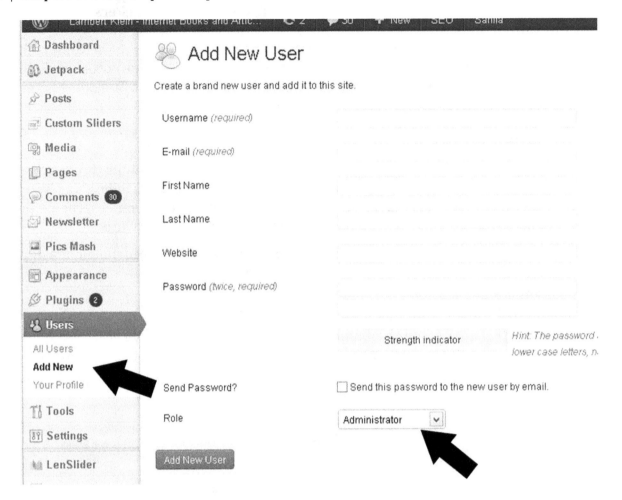

Online Threats

While offline threats are probably the greatest threat to your WordPress security, online threats can be just as dangerous if you're unprepared. Online attacks can come in many different forms, from corrupt plugins that rewrite your files to SQL injection attacks to brute force password hacking. Fortunately, for every hacking technique, there are countermeasures to prevent it.

File Permissions

Certain files in your WordPress folders are "write–accessible." This means that anyone who can access them can rewrite them; no special permissions are needed. While this is necessary in many cases to allow your WordPress site to function (some plugins rewrite files), there are certain files that need to have this disabled for security purposes.

Take a look at this list of files that should not be writable:

⚔ The root directory (except .htaccess, if you want WordPress to automatically configure rewrite rules for you)

⚔ /wp-admin/

⚔ /wp-includes/

⚔ /wp-content/plugins/

Keep in mind that /wp-content/ itself should be writable. Making it unwritable could cause problems.

To change a file from writable to unwritable, it is easiest to use a FTP program such as Filezilla, although you can do this via your cPanel as well. To do this in Filezilla, all you have to do is right-click the file you want to alter and select "File Attributes." A new window will pop up that will allow you to change the permissions. Unclick the boxes that say "Write" for both Group and Public. This will ensure that only those with admin access can rewrite these files. Go through and do this for all the files listed above and any others you don't want to be writable.

Plugin Threats

Plugins are a handy way to change the functionality of your WordPress site and make it easier to use. While 99.9% of plugins are safe to use, there are some out there that have been designed by hackers to exploit your system. As previously mentioned, some plugins actively rewrite some of your WordPress files to function, and this can lead to a security breach. Though the risk of being hacked by a bogus plugin is very small, you can decrease your chances even further by following a few simple steps.

The first and most obvious way to prevent a bad plugin from allowing a hacker access to your system is to only download plugins from trusted sources. When you find a plugin, either through using the WordPress plugin search or a search engine like Google, you want to make sure that it comes from a reputable source.

Look for signs that the plugin is the real deal. Does the plugin have a lot of good ratings? Does it have a website explaining how it works? A hacker's plugin will often times have no effort put into the webpage where you download it, and it won't have any ratings since it is just a cheap attempt to hack people's WordPress accounts. If you are unsure about a plugin that you want, do a Google search to see if other people are talking about it or have discovered that it is a hacker plugin.

Scanning plugins for viruses and Trojans is another way to ensure that your system isn't exploited. To do this, don't download a plugin directly from the WordPress search, but instead go to the download page and download it onto your hard drive. You can then use your anti-virus/anti-malware software to scan the file and confirm that it doesn't contain any nasty surprises. It is recommended that you do this for themes as well, since they too can contain malicious code.

Keep in mind that just because a plugin is free from viruses and malware doesn't mean that it can't exploit your system. A hacker plugin may be built to exploit your system without the use of viruses, Trojans or stuff like that. This is why it is important to make sure you're only downloading plugins that are trustworthy.

Another bit of advice is to always make sure that your plugins are kept up-to-date. An out-of-date plugin can pose a security risk because, as hackers improve their hacking techniques, WordPress, plugins and other security systems have to evolve as well. If you have any inactive plugins on your WordPress site, delete them to ensure that they aren't used as an exploitation method.

Computer Vulnerability

We'll get into this a bit later when we discuss how to protect your computer from viruses, malware and more, but I just need to explain why this is important. When your WordPress site is attacked, the hacker doesn't necessarily have to target the site itself or even your web hosting server. If your computer has no virus protection or firewall, the hacker can get in that way as well.

If your computer becomes compromised by a hacker, this then opens the door for him or her to get into everything, including your WordPress site and web hosting. One of the most important rules of protecting your WordPress site is to ensure that your computer's security is top-notch. Lock your computer down with the latest virus protection, firewall and other security features to make sure that it isn't compromised by a hacker.

Router Security

Another major threat to your WordPress security, and your computer's security as a whole, is your router. This is especially true if you're using a wireless connection, as it is very easy for external sources to "piggyback" onto your network.

Piggybacking causes several problems aside from being a major security hazard. If you pay for your Internet connection per Gigabyte, the intruder will increase your monthly bill. Having an intruder on your network will also decrease your connection speed as well.

One of the main ways hackers exploit a wireless connection is via packet sniffing. This technique scans the data passing through your wireless network for cookies, passwords, usernames, HTTP requests and much more. Any sensitive data could potentially be intercepted and exploited.

The first thing you're going to want to do to prevent this from happening is to change your router's username and password. Hackers are crafty individuals and can get lists of default usernames and passwords for virtually any router in existence. Leaving your username and password as default is like leaving the key to your house sitting on your doormat.

Username and Password

In most cases, you can access your router's setup screen by typing "192.168.1.1" into your browser. (The IP address could be different, such as 192.168.3.1. Check your router's documentation.) You will then be prompted to enter your username and password. If you are unsure of what they are, try checking the manual your router came with. If for some reason you can't get this to work, then do a Google search for more info or contact the manufacturer. In any case, make sure you get that username and password changed as soon as possible.

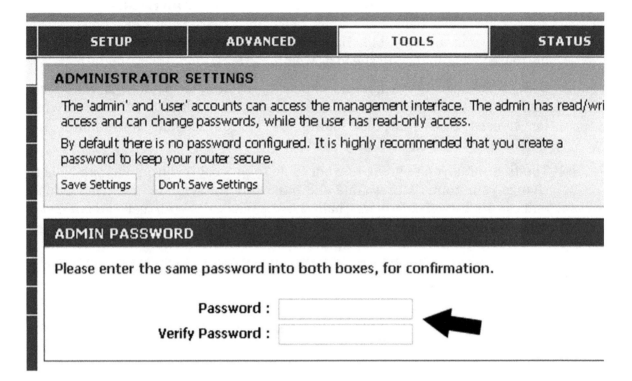

SSID

Another thing you're going to want to do while you're in your router's admin area is change the SSID name, which is basically the name of your network. In most cases, this will simply be listed as "default" or as the name of the manufacturer of your router. Changing this won't necessarily give you additional protection against hackers but it will ensure that no one accesses your network by accident.

SETUP	ADVANCED	TOOLS	S

WIRELESS

Wireless Network Settings

Use this section to configure the wireless settings for your D-Link Router. Please note changes made on this section may also need to be duplicated on your Wireless Clier

[Save Settings]   [Don't Save Settings]

WIRELESS NETWORK SETTINGS

Enable Wireless : ☑

Wireless Network Name : thinkhealthy   (Also called the SSID)

Enable Auto Channel Scan : ☑

Wireless Channel : 2.437 GHz - CH 6

802.11 Mode : Mixed 802.11ng, 802.11g and 802.11b

Transmission Rate : Best (automatic)   (Mbit/s)

Channel Width : Auto 20/40 MHz

Visibility Status : ◉ Visible ○ Invisible

WIRELESS SECURITY MODE

To protect your privacy you can configure wireless security features. This device supp wireless security modes, including WEP, WPA-Personal, and WPA-Enterprise. WEP is wireless encryption standard. WPA provides a higher level of security. WPA-Personal require an authentication server. The WPA-Enterprise option requires an external RAD

Security Mode : None

For example, if you and a neighbor both have Linksys routers and your signals are overlapping, there is the possibility that they could get on your network by accident or vice versa. This could slow down your connection and increase your monthly bill, as described earlier.

WEP/WPA2 Encryption

You'll want to make sure you enable encryption while in your router's admin page, as well. This will make it much harder for others to encroach onto your network. To do this, set the network to use either WEP or WPA2 encryption methods. If your router is older than 2006, use WEP. If it was made in 2006 or later, use WPA2, which is more secure but incompatible with older routers. In most cases, you will also be prompted to enter a password. Make it something hard to guess, such as a random string of numbers, symbols and letters.

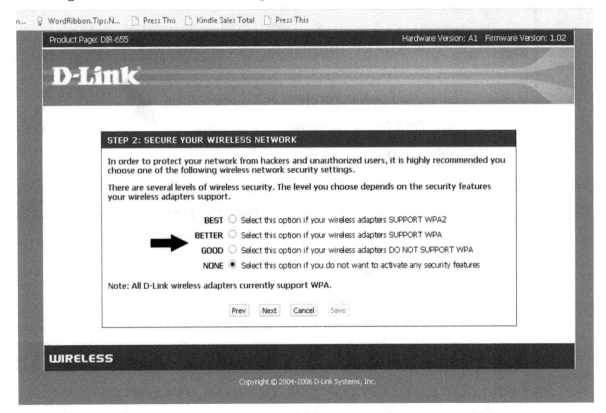

MAC Address Filtering

Each wireless device, from laptops to smart phones, has what is known as a MAC address, which is like an IP address for wireless use. To ensure that unauthorized devices don't access your router, you can make it so that only pre-approved devices are allowed to connect to it. This is because MAC addresses are hard-coded into your networking equipment, so that one address only lets one single device connect to the network.

The first step to pulling this off is to decide which devices you want to allow connecting to your wireless network. Once that's done, you need to get the MAC addresses of all these devices. To find this on a computer, you'd typically open up the command prompt and type in "ipconfig/all." This will show the MAC address beside where it says "Physical Address."

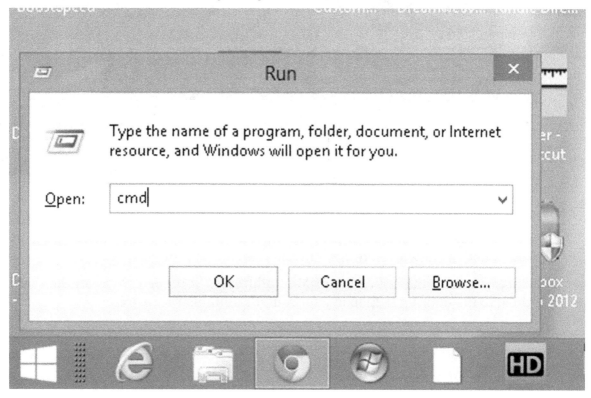

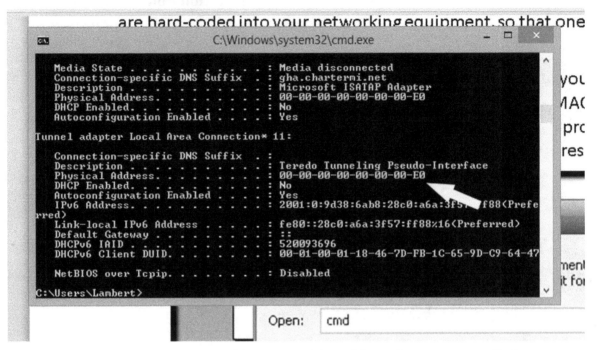

For smart phones and other portable devices like tablets, this can generally be found under "network settings," though this can vary for each device.

Once you have the entire list of MAC addresses you need, you can then add them to the filtering section in your router's administrative area.

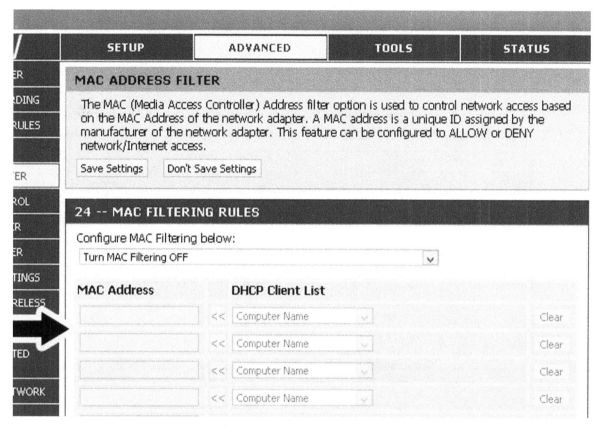

Reducing the Signal Range

Most routers typically have a pretty large wireless range. This can work to your disadvantage, especially if you live in an apartment complex. Fortunately, it is easy to deal with this by changing the mode of your router from 802.11n or 802.11b to 802.11g. You can also use a different wireless channel.

Other, simpler methods include wrapping tinfoil around your router's antenna, placing the router in a box or even hiding it under the bed. Keep in mind that these methods can sometimes cause signal interference.

Another method is to use anti-WiFi paint.

`http://news.bbc.co.uk/2/hi/8279549.stm`

Yes, such a thing actually exists. This special paint is designed to absorb radio signals and would easily confine your router's signal to a single room if the walls were covered with it. This could be especially useful in an apartment complex... though you'd need to get permission from the property manager first, of course.

Firmware Upgrades and Updates

Just like most other security software, your router's firmware will need to be updated on occasion to counteract the evolving techniques of hackers. Check in at your router manufacturer's website occasionally to see if there are any new updates available.

To check which version of firmware your router is currently running, access your router's dashboard at 192.168.1.1, then go to the firmware section.

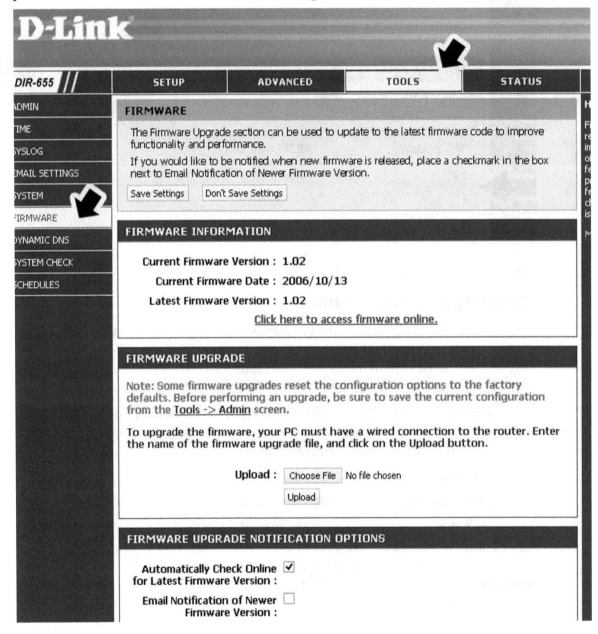

Other Prevention Tactics

Now that you understand some of the basics when it comes to protecting your WordPress site and your computer from both offline and online threats, let's get into some of the other ways you can protect yourself from hackers. Some of these techniques are a bit on the technical side, but ultimately pretty easy to pull off.

Update WordPress and Plugins

As mentioned a few times, hackers are constantly evolving their techniques to crack into WordPress. To counter this, WordPress continuously improves their software, as well. This makes it very important to update WordPress as soon as possible when a new version comes out.

Also, make sure that you're updating your plugins when they need to be updated. Frequent updating combined with deleting unused plugins will help to ensure that they are not exploited and used by a hacker to gain access to your site.

Backing Up Your Websites and Databases

We're going to get into how to create and backup SQL databases a bit farther down the road, but for now I just want to get across the importance of doing it. This is actually more of a "damage control" technique than an anti-hacking technique.

In a worst-case scenario, if you get hacked, the hacker may decide to completely wipe your data when they're done doing whatever it is they broke into your WordPress site to do. This can destroy months or even years of hard work. This is why your website needs to be backed up.

Backing up your website is pretty simple and typically consists of either using a plugin to do it, manually backing up the SQL database you created, or both. I'll go into this in more detail later. I recommend having multiple databases for multiple sites, so that if a hacker gets into one website, they can't also get into every site on your server.

Your web hosting should back up your data as well if they're doing their job. Before you purchase web hosting, make sure you verify that they do this for you. Most companies, like Host Gator and Bluehost, do this automatically at regular intervals.

.htaccess Lock-Down

Your .htaccess file is one of your most important files when it comes to WordPress security. By default, it is at risk of being exploited by cunning hackers, but a few simple changes will make it much more secure and prevent people from using it to invade your WordPress site.

The first thing you should do is make a copy of your .htaccess file. When editing files, you can sometimes screw things up and render your entire website inoperable. This will ensure that if something goes wrong, you can re-upload the original file and start over.

To find the .htaccessfile for the root domain, you're going to go from the root folder down to the public_html folder and look in there. The file will be below any add-on domains you may have and folders like wp_admin.

To access the .htaccess file for add-on domains, you have to click the folder for that add-on domain that's in your public_html file under the root folder.

Keep in mind that the contents of your .htaccess file may differ a bit between your root domain and your add-on domains. Also, sometimes your .htaccess file will be hidden, and you'll have to select "Show Hidden Files." In Filezilla, this is done by clicking on "Server" then "Force showing hidden files."

Editing your .htaccess file can have a variety of results, some of which can be unpredictable, depending on which folder you place it in. Some web hosting companies may not provide you with .htaccess files, so you may have to create them yourself, which is relatively simple.

To create a .htaccess file, simply open a text editor like Notepad and paste in the following:

```
# BEGIN WordPress
<ifmodule mod_rewrite.c>
RewriteEngine On
RewriteBase /
RewriteCond %{REQUEST_FILENAME} !-f
RewriteCond %{REQUEST_FILENAME} !-d
RewriteRule . /index.php [L]
</ifmodule>
# END WordPress
```

Save the file as ".htaccess" and upload it into the folder of your choice. This will typically be the public_html folder, but it can go in other folders, too, such as the main folder for each add-on domain.

Protecting Your wp-admin Folder

The next thing you want to do is limit which IP addresses can access the admin area of your WordPress site. This will ensure that even if they crack your username and password, a hacker can't get into your admin area. Keep in mind that a side effect of this will be that you will also be unable to access your admin area from any computer that is not listed in the file.

To do this, go into your .htaccess file by right-clicking on it and selecting "view/edit." Then, add the following code:

```
AuthUserFile /dev/null

AuthGroupFile /dev/null

AuthName "Access Control"

AuthType Basic

order deny,allow

deny from all

#IP address to Whitelist

allow from 123.456.789.012
```

(Swap out the IP address 123.456.789.012 with your own IP address.)

You can add other IP addresses as well if you have multiple devices you want to grant access to, or if you have other trusted individuals who need to access your site from their computers.

An alternate, simpler code you can use is:

```
# deny access to wp admin
order deny,allow
allow from xx.xx.xx.xx #
deny from all
```

Replace the "xx"s with your static IP.

This technique is only viable if you use a static IP address. A dynamic address, which changes constantly, won't work here because this limits access to your admin folder to specific IP addresses.

Protection .hta Files

You can also strengthen your .htaccess file by adding the following code to your domain's root .htaccess file:

```
# STRONG HTACCESS PROTECTION</code>
<Files ~ "^.*\.([Hh][Tt][Aa])">
order allow,deny
deny from all
satisfy all
</Files>
```

What this does is prevent any external access to files that have .hta, drastically decreasing the chances of an external source hacking these files.

While you're doing this, you also need to limit your .htaccess file's write access. In your FTP client, you can simply enter the numeric value 644. This will give the following permissions:

Owner: Read, Write

Group: Read

Public: Read

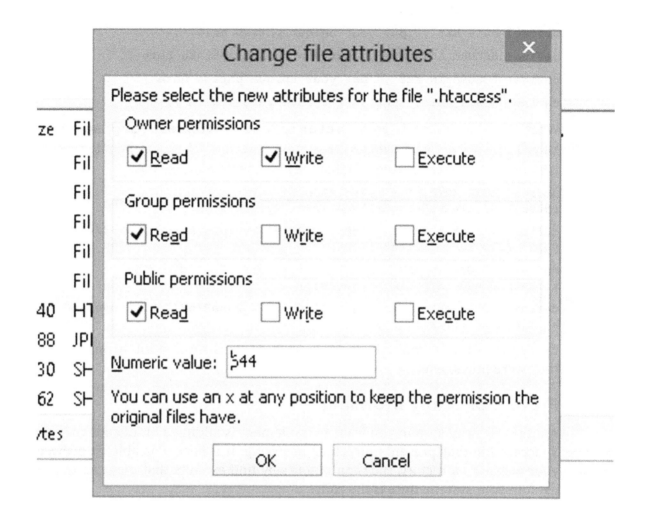

Protect Your wp-config.php File

You can also secure your wp-config.php file by adding this code at the very bottom of your htaccess file:

```
<Files wp-config.php>
Order Deny,Allow
Deny from All
</Files>
```

Ideally, you should do both, as this will also help to limit unauthorized access to your wp_config.php file.

Another method of protecting this file is through adding custom security keys. When you get into your wp-config file, you'll find a section that looks like this:

```
define('AUTH_KEY', 'put your unique phrase here');

define('SECURE_AUTH_KEY', 'put your unique phrase here');

define('LOGGED_IN_KEY', 'put your unique phrase here');

define('NONCE_KEY', 'put your unique phrase here');
```

What you want to do is go to **https://api.wordpress.org/secret-key/1.1/** and get your own secret security keys. You'll then use them to replace the bottom four "define" rules, so that they look something like this:

```
define('AUTH_KEY','lj+_ .[6c1=13n
rhZBhjXdOo|miL<baCpYhqZrl}o2a|irZy-]Wy8PYW+a]zE]5');

define('SECURE_AUTH_KEY','s8p1+WgH0{Ph/)Vr;pFggsp{xoh8Cy>>#/+]EJ|P|
yQfS* /SJO7XuK#G3&f1rnZ');

define('LOGGED_IN_KEY','h$eIl%#nZ|.}z-U)Z:O$u,y c[N;7^j-
x,)Zs*wUHheGO-(KKpONVC664X$uO$Mt');

define('NONCE_KEY','d=>/Uh@%RnZ|*<bGq[2<_R@spP*oE[7oE?<#%xyoowmU0Xz
xK DjhyLXLcifX32k');
```

Encryption of user data will make your login passwords a lot stronger than they were previously.

Prevent Directory Browsing

Another security system you want to implement is adding a bit of code to your .htaccess file that prevents directory browsing. If a hacker is able to browse your website's directory, they can potentially find exploits that they can use to get into your system. Here is the code:

```
# disable directory browsing
Options All -Indexes
```

Put that into your .htaccess file in the root directory of your website.

Protecting Your wp-content File

Your wp-content folder is very important and can contain a lot of sensitive data. To ensure that this data isn't compromised, locate the .htaccess file in your wp-content folder (not the root .htaccess file) and add this code:

```
Order deny,allow
Deny from all
<Files ~ ".(xml|css|jpe?g|png|gif|js)$">
Allow from all
</Files>
```

As you can see, it is somewhat similar to the code that protects your wp_config.php file. If there isn't a .htaccess file in your wp-content folder, simply create one with the above code and any other security code you want in it.

Preventing Script Injections

Script injection is a sneaky way hackers can get into your files using an SQL exploit. The good news is that there is a very easy way to prevent this. Just paste the following code into your .htaccess file in your root folder.

```
# protect from sql injection
Options +FollowSymLinks
RewriteEngine On
RewriteCond %{QUERY_STRING} (\<|%3C).*script.*(\>|%3E) [NC,OR]
RewriteCond %{QUERY_STRING} GLOBALS(=|\[|\%[0-9A-Z]{0,2}) [OR]
RewriteCond %{QUERY_STRING} _REQUEST(=|\[|\%[0-9A-Z]{0,2})
RewriteRule ^(.*)$ index.php [F,L]
```

Another way to help prevent script injections is to change the prefix of your tables. By default, the prefix is "wp_"... and every hacker knows that. The prefix can be easily changed by using the WP Security Scan plugin. Browse to this URL **http://wordpress.org/extend/plugins/wp-security-scan/** to visit the download page for more info.

Keep Search Engines from Indexing Your Admin Area

Google and other search engines have very efficient crawlers that go through your site and index its pages. Unfortunately, they can also end up indexing your admin area if you're not careful.

To prevent this, you're going to want to create a robots.txt file to place in your root directory. The file should contain the following code:

```
Disallow: /wp-*
```

 Browse to http://www.robotstxt.org/robotstxt.html for more detailed information on how to create and configure a robots.txt file and where it goes.

Delete Inactive User Accounts

This should go without saying. If you have user accounts on your WordPress site that no one uses, they should be deleted. Accounts created by users other than you can have weak username and password security that can be potentially exploited and used by hackers to gain entry into your site.

Using HTTPS

While most sites use HTTP, sites that need extra security, such as payment processors like PayPal, use HTTPS. This is an improved version of HTTP that you can use on your site for additional security.

By using HTTPS, your username and password will be encrypted, ensuring that they are lot harder to decode if they happen to be intercepted by a hacker.

There are two basic ways to enable HTTPS on your site. The first is the manual way, which is done by adding the following code to your wp-config.php file:

```
define('FORCE_SSL_LOGIN', true);
```

The other method is by using the plugin Admin-SSL, which you can get by Browsing to http://www.kerrins.co.uk/blog/admin-ssl/ . It's free, so I encourage you to donate to the creator if you choose to use it.

Security Plugins

I've already mentioned a couple of plugins you can use to beef up your security. Here I'll go down a complete list of all the best security plugins you can use on your WordPress site. Remember to always keep your plugins up-to-date!

Browse to the following URLs for links to the download pages for these plugins.

WP Security Scan

```
http://wordpress.org/extend/plugins/wp-security-scan/
```

Scans your WordPress installation for security vulnerabilities, exploits, and anything else you should know about. It also suggests corrective measures you can use to beef up your security.

Admin-SSL

```
http://wordpress.org/extend/plugins/admin-ssl-secure-admin/
```

Uses private SSL protocols so secure your login page, admin area, and more. This allows you to use HTTPS for maximum encryption of sensitive data.

WordPress FireWall2

```
http://wordpress.org/extend/plugins/wordpress-firewall-2/
```

Protect your WordPress site with a powerful firewall. This plugin is an updated version of the popular WordPress FireWall.

Bulletproof Security

```
http://wordpress.org/extend/plugins/bulletproof-security/
```

This is a high-end security plugin for WordPress that protects against XSS, CSRF, SQL Injection and much more. This is a great alternative to manually configuring your .htaccess files if you struggle with that.

WP-DB-Backup

`http://wordpress.org/extend/plugins/wp-db-backup/`

If a hacker attacks, you'll find how essential it is to have a backup of your data. This plugin also allows you to back up other tables within the same database.

Antispam Bee

`http://wordpress.org/extend/plugins/antispam-bee/`

A cutting-edge anti-spam plugin. This program eliminates incoming spam by analyzing it thoroughly, including the ping. This plugin is also anonymous and registration-free.

SI CAPTCHA Anti-Spam

`http://wordpress.org/extend/plugins/si-captcha-for-wordpress/`

Fight off spambots with this handy plugin, which adds a captcha form to your comments section, login page and more. Works incredibly well with Akismet, another popular anti-spam plugin.

Blackhole

`http://perishablepress.com/blackhole-bad-bots/`

Having a robots.txt file in your root directory sometimes isn't quite good enough. Blackhole traps any bots that make it past your robots.txt file. This sophisticated software also does a WHOIS lookup on the bad bots and records their activity, so that all future bots of the same origin are permanently denied access to your files.

AskApache Password Protect

`http://wordpress.org/extend/plugins/askapache-password-protect/`

This plugin is designed to add multiple layers of security to your website. By using additional password protection, you can build a virtual "wall" of defense around your webslte.

TAC (Theme Authenticy Checker)

`http://wordpress.org/extend/plugins/tac/`

Did you know that viruses, exploit kits and more can be sneaked in with themes as well as plugins? This plugin checks the source files of all your installed themes for malicious code and other bad stuff.

Antivirus

`http://wordpress.org/extend/plugins/antivirus/`

This plugin constantly checks for dangerous viruses, malware and exploits designed specifically to target WordPress. It also comes with multilingual support.

WP Email Guard

`http://wordpress.org/extend/plugins/wp-email-guard/`

Worried about your email address being scraped off of your website by bots? This plugin converts all of your emails within the body of your posts to Javacode, making it readable only by real humans and not malicious bots.

WordPress File Monitor

`http://wordpress.org/extend/plugins/wordpress-file-monitor/`

Manually monitoring your WordPress files for any signs of hacking is a chore. This plugin will monitor your WordPress files for any additions, changes or deletions. When a change is detected, you can have the plugin email you.

Ultimate Security Checker

`http://wordpress.org/extend/plugins/ultimate-security-checker/`

This plugin scans your WordPress installation for literally hundreds of known security threats, and then gives you a security rating based on how well protected you are.

Outsourcing WordPress Security

A lot of this security stuff for WordPress is somewhat technical. The good news is that these tasks can be outsourced; there are several different ways to go about this.

The first way is to hire a professional computer security firm to take care of this for you. These firms typically range in price from moderate to expensive. This is a case of "you get what you pay for," though, and your site will be ultra-secure if you choose this route. The only problem is that it may not be economically feasible for you unless you run your own business.

Another way to do this is to hire a freelancer from a site like Freelancer.com. These freelancers typically charge less, but are still adequately knowledgeable about WordPress security and can lock up your site pretty tightly. If you feel the need, you can pay your freelancer to do monthly or weekly security checks on your site. In fact, in most cases, the only things you'll be missing out on by hiring a freelancer rather than a security firm are advanced software solutions for security issues and 24/7 systems monitoring.

Chapter 3: Computer Virus Protection

There are all sorts of programs out on the Web that can get into your computer and mess you up. Viruses, spyware, adware, Trojans and worms are a few types, and they can be difficult to remove without the right tools. The best option is to install the proper protection software and keep your system safe from the beginning.

When protecting your WordPress site, it's very important to keep your entire computer or network secure. An infected file on your computer could corrupt your website's data; a key-logger hiding in your system could give your passwords away to a hacker.

The more you understand about virus protection, the better equipped you will be for defending yourself and your data.

Keep your System Updated

Windows operating systems have automatic update features that allow you to download the latest security patches for your OS. These come straight from Microsoft and should be installed as soon as possible.

Microsoft has gotten pretty good at keeping their systems secure and Apple computers are inherently much harder to hack or infect with malicious programs. Because of this, many malicious programmers choose to get through to your data by exploiting weaknesses in the browsers you use. This means it is important to keep your browser up-to-date as well.

Many browsers tell you right away when there is a new version out. Some will even update automatically.

Holes in a browser aren't the only way to get into your system. Popular plugins like Adobe Flash Player are constantly under attack from new viruses, which can also leave you exposed. Update your plugins regularly. As with browsers and system updates, these will usually notify you when there's a new version released.

Windows OS also has programs such as Windows Defender that act as basic anti-virus tools. Windows Defender can be helpful, but it shouldn't be the only program you rely on. Windows Defender isn't updated nearly as often as a commercial security program would be because it isn't intended to be your main defense. Find quality anti-virus and anti-malware programs, or you could find yourself dealing with difficult system-damaging traps.

What to Buy

How do you know which virus protection you should buy? There are many different programs you can buy, so you need to know what you want in software security.

Your first task is to find a product with all the features you need. Here is what you're looking for when shopping:

- ⋏ Real-time Scanner: This feature actively scans all data that comes through your network. It can find and quarantine viruses and malware before they hide or install themselves in your system.

- ⋏ Heuristic Scanner: This process helps catch viruses and other programs that might not be in the software's virus database yet. It uses what it knows about other malicious programs to find new threats and contain them before damage can spread.

- ⋏ POP3 Email and Webmail Scanner: It should be able to detect malicious programs in attachments both on POP3 email programs and web-based mail systems like Hotmail or Gmail.

- ⋏ Instant Message Protection: Sometimes, worms and other programs will try to get into your system through instant message clients via infected computers on your contact list. A decent security software package will be able to block this.

- ⋏ Scheduled Scans: Set your protection software to run an automated scan on specified days or times. It's important to run full scans frequently in case something has managed to sneak past the real-time scanner.

- ⋏ Script Blocking: Scripts may be used to execute harmful programs on your computer through the browser. Your software should be able to identify harmful scripts and stop them.

- ⋏ Automatic Updates: Thousands of new viruses are written every day. Keeping your software up-to-date is a high priority, and automatic updates make that easy.

The next thing to keep in mind is the cost. Some protection programs are subscription based, while others have a one-time fee for security. There are even some free options available online. While you shouldn't put your security at risk to save some money, there are quality programs available that are either cheap or free.

Additionally, some programs have basic packages but offer better protection for a higher cost. Make sure that the price you choose gives you all the features you need. You don't want to buy software thinking you're getting the whole package when you actually only got half.

Configure your Protection

Once you've selected your protection and installed it, you'll want to configure it. You may be tempted to just let it do what it wants, but you'll quickly find that anti-virus software needs to be customized. If you don't tell it what to do, you could end up not activating the features you need, or even have safe software blocked.

Read the Manual

Many people neglect the manual when they first open a new product. They go by an "I can figure it out myself" mentality that can lead them to problems. Now, you don't have to sit down and read the instructions front to back, but when you come up to something you're having trouble with, it should be the first place you look.

If you bought your program in a box, it should come with a paper manual that can answer some basic questions you may have. Some even come with a digital manual located on a disk in the box. If the manual doesn't help you ,or you downloaded your software online, go to the company's website. They will most likely have an FAQ, knowledge base, or support system that can help. Online directions and support are likely to be the most up-to-date instructions you'll find.

Basic Configuration

Start with the automatic scanner. You want to be sure this is set to run at a time when your computer will be on, but you won't be working. For example, if your scanner is set to run at midnight, but you turn your computer off at 11:00 PM every night, this may prevent your anti-virus from finding an infection. Also, you don't want to run the scanner while you're working, as that can slow your computer's performance greatly.

The automatic updater needs to be set to check for updates every day, which is the default setting for most programs. Some programs will allow you to check for updates several times a day. You want to have the latest updates for your systems, and new updates could be published at any time. The more often you update, the safer you will be, but once a day is usually fine.

You also need to become familiar with your whitelist, which is composed of software you want your security systems to leave alone. Security programs can sometimes interfere with or block software you use regularly by mistaking it for a threat. If this happens, you'll need to know how to tell the program that this software is safe. Also, you will want to make sure that all the features you need are enabled. Some may be disabled by default.

Chapter 4: Backing Up your Website's Data

Imagine that one day, you go to your website and find the entire thing has been ransacked by a hacker. Your database has been destroyed and there's nothing left of your hard work. Now imagine that you hadn't taken the time to back up your disks and there's no way to get your data back.

What if your hard drive malfunctioned because your system overheated? Or maybe you were in the middle of moving and someone dropped your computer down a flight of stairs. What would you do?

Life happens. These scenarios are entirely possible, which is exactly why you need to take the extra steps to back up and secure your data. The first step to do so is to decide on a method. How are you going to do it?

Remember, your web host will have backups of your data on their servers, but for extra security, you may want to create your own. If something were to happen to their building, such as a fire or a flood, you could lose your server and your backups. Also, if they go out of business and you haven't made your own copies, you could lose all of your data without warning.

One method you could use would be to upload your files to cloud storage, which is an increasingly popular option right now. For a more down-to-earth choice, there's also RAID configuration through multiple hard drives, as well as NAS systems. If you have a large budget and need the extra safety, you could decide to combine some of these methods.

Let's take a look at these storage methods.

Cloud Storage

Cloud storage is incredibly popular. It's easy to use and gives you access to your files anywhere with an Internet connection. If you have a lot of files you need stored, it can save you a lot of money.

Storing your backup "in the cloud" basically means uploading your data to a remote server. That server is regularly backed up so the company won't lose your data in the event of a malfunction.

Cloud services usually charge a monthly or yearly subscription fee. Some offer discounts for larger purchases. Some services put a limit on how much storage you can have, but there are unlimited options available that you should look for. You'll want to shop around and see what the best deals are.

Cloud storage is great because you don't have to deal with maintenance and upkeep for the storage servers. You never have to worry about upgrading your storage hardware, either.

If you work across multiple computers, you can set up your cloud storage to automatically sync to your computers. That way, you can have access to everything you need, no matter what computer you are using.

You should keep security in mind, and cloud storage does offer encryption to help keep your information safe. However, the more remote servers there are that hold your data, the more you risk having your data compromised. A disgruntled or unethical employee could turn your data out to someone else.

Remember, storing data on a cloud server means that you're sharing your data with at least one other person. The fewer people you have handling your data, the more secure it will be. If you have confidential documents, you may want to consider storing the data yourself, or make sure you find a storage solution that doesn't compromise your privacy or that of your clients/users/etc.

Cloud storage companies are also not immune to damage, just like the rest of the world. If a fire were to destroy the building and equipment that stored your data, your backups would be gone. In addition, if the company were to go bankrupt, you could lose your data without any warning.

Extra Hard Drives

If you want more options, you can also buy an extra hard drive for your system. Running your own hard drives can give you extra security and control over your data. You can also set up your hard drives so that your entire network has access to them.

Your hard drive will likely come with software to help automate your backups. This software can update your backup as soon as the original file is saved. You don't have to worry about whether or not you uploaded the latest changes to your backup.

Of course, adding your own hard drives isn't without its own fair share of problems. If there is a technical issue, it's your responsibility to get it fixed. This could mean spending time finding the solution yourself, or hiring someone to do it.

Another problem with maintaining your own backups is that it can be costly. Hard drives themselves can cost hundreds of dollars. You will also need to upgrade them every few years or so, as they become old and slow. You will have to pay for the extra electricity to run these servers, as well.

If you only plan to run one or two extra drives, or you don't need a lot of space, then the costs may not be so bad. In fact, it may even turn out to be cheaper than renting space on a cloud server for years. However, if you have a lot of valuable data you need to back up, then the price tag will increase quite a bit.

Picking a Hard Disk

When choosing a brand of hard drives, you'll want to keep some things in mind:

How much storage do you need? You don't want to buy more than you'll need. You may think that you'll fill it eventually, but keep in mind that technology ages very quickly and you may need to upgrade sooner than you expect. Any disk space not used by the time you upgrade was wasted money.

Do I want an internal or external drive? Internal drives don't require any extra desk space; all you need is the right cords and connectors inside your machine. External hard drives give you portability and are easy to install, but require more physical space.

How do I install this? If you aren't familiar with installing new hardware into your computer, you'll need to find some instructions to help you out. If you aren't comfortable taking your computer apart yourself, you can take your system into a shop and have a technician do it. However, they may charge you quite a bit for a relatively easy procedure.

What is the failure rate for this drive? You don't want to buy a drive that isn't going to last. For example, if you decide you want to buy a solid-state drive, it would be helpful to know that these have a higher failure rate than hard disks.

Set Up a RAID

A more advanced option is to set up your own system and store your data across multiple disks. You can link multiple hard drives together on your system to create a RAID (Redundant Array of Independent Disks). A RAID uses special software to spread your data across multiple drives. If a drive fails, then the other drives would be able to restore the lost data.

The cost of a RAID depends on how many hard disks you include and what size storage they are. However, the benefits may be worth the cost. When you're in control of your storage, there are automatically fewer people who have access to your data. Remember, the fewer people involved, the more secure it is.

Network Attached Storage Devices

What if you had personal cloud storage—a device that you could set up for your own private network that was wireless and could connect all your devices? If this sounds good to you, then maybe a network attached storage (NAS) device is what you're looking for.

An NAS device uses RAID technology to keep your data safe. You connect it to your own network and assign it an IP address of its own. Then, you can connect to the device easily. You can also set up user profiles with password protection and even data encryption to help stay secure.

Creating SQL Databases

In addition to backing up your WordPress site itself, you are also going to want to back up your SQL database. This has the additional benefit of allowing you to restore lost data in the event of a hack. You may remember this from my previous guide, WordPress Domination.

You can find it at: **http://www.amazon.com/dp/B007LS0TLE**

Creating an SQL database is pretty easy, but the steps you take may differ depending on who your web hosting company is. In WordPress Domination, I went over how to do this with Host Gator. This time, I'm going to show you how to do it with Bluehost, since they are a popular web hosting company, too.

Start off by selecting "My SQL Database" on your cPanel. It will have a little dolphin picture on the icon.

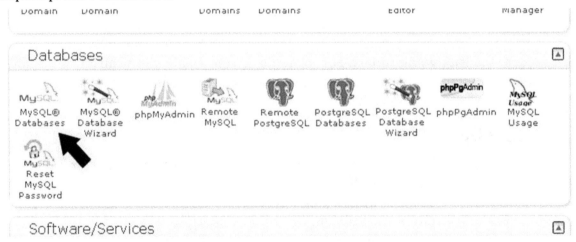

On the next screen, enter the name of your new database. It can be whatever you want, but there will be a character limit. Also, your cPanel username will be added to the front of this database name automatically upon creation. Once you're done, click "Create Database."

Create New Database

New Database: ██████ [_____]

Create Database

Once it is on there, click the "Go Back" button on the next screen to return to the previous screen. Now, we need to create an SQL user, so scroll down to the part that says "Add New User." Enter any username you want, but be aware that this too will have your cPanel username added to the front of it.

Next, you need to create your password. Refer to the passwords chapter later in this guide for more details on how to create ultra-secure passwords.

When you're done, click "Create User."

MySQL Users
Add New User

Username: ██████ _ [_____]

Password: [_____]

Password (Again): [_____]

Strength (why?): [Very Weak (0/100)]   Password Generator

Create User

The last thing you're going to do is link the username you just created with the database you just created. Scroll down to where it says "Add User to Database." Now, select the user and database and hit "Add."

Add User To Database

User: ▼

Database: ▼

Add

On the next page, select "All permission," then click the "Make Changes" button.

☐ **ALL PRIVILEGES**	
☐ ALTER	☐ ALTER ROUTINE
☐ CREATE	☐ CREATE ROUTINE
☐ CREATE TEMPORARY TABLES	☐ CREATE VIEW
☐ DELETE	☐ DROP
☐ EXECUTE	☐ INDEX
☐ INSERT	☐ LOCK TABLES
☐ REFERENCES	☐ SELECT
☐ SHOW VIEW	☐ TRIGGER
☐ UPDATE	

Make Changes

See how easy that was?

Browse here `http://www.youtube.com/watch?v=mtQqg_I_oZ0` for a video tutorial so you can watch how this is done on Bluehost. If you have a different hosting company, the steps you follow will probably be similar.

Browse to `https://my.bluehost.com/cgi/help/5` **for a link on how to back up an SQL database on Bluehost and** `https://my.bluehost.com/cgi/help/4` **for how to restore an SQL database on Bluehost. Also, you can go to** `http://support.hostgator.com/articles/cpanel/how-to-backuprestore-your-mysql-database` **for info on how to back up and restore an SQL database using Host Gator.**

Optimally, you should create an SQL database for every WordPress installation on your server. This will ensure that if a hacker gets into one site, they won't have immediate access to your other sites.

Chapter 5: You've Been Hacked! Damage Control 101

Sometimes, no matter how much security you put on your WordPress site, a hacker gets in. Though these situations are rare, they do happen, and you should be prepared to deal with this in order to minimize the damage.

Finding the Source of the Hack

The very first thing to do if you have been hacked is to find out how the intruder got into your site. They could have gotten in from an infection in your computer itself, so that is one of the best places to start. Run a scan of your entire computer to see if you find any Trojans, root-kits, viruses or any other malicious software that could have been responsible for the hack.

If you find that your computer has been hacked, it is suggested that you look up info online as to how to handle the situation. Browse here `http://www.switched.com/2011/02/23/what-to-do-if-your-pc-gets-hacked/` for some info to get you started.

If the hack came from an infected plugin, SQL injection or another attack that went after your WordPress site directly, you'll need to check with your hosting provider. They can confirm whether or not it was an actual hack and tell you what you should do.

Changing Your Passwords

Once you've determined the source of the hack, you should immediately change your passwords. This includes those for your website, your FTP, your SQL databases and your cPanel. If you really want to play it safe, you can change your password for every place online where you need one.

If your computer itself was hacked, it is recommended that you change the passwords on all your user accounts. In some cases, you may even want to delete your user account and create a new one. Keep in mind that this should be done *after* you have confirmed that your computer, server, website and everything else are no longer compromised and are fully protected from repeated hacking attempts.

Also, be sure to check your WordPress user's area. Make sure the hacker didn't create a new user, especially one with admin privileges.

Upgrade to the Latest WordPress Version

If you haven't already done so, upgrade WordPress to the most recent version. This will ensure that, if the hacker took advantage of an outdated WordPress version, they won't be able to attack your system the same way again.

Another thing you're going to want to do is change the secret keys for your WordPress site. These are the randomized keys that you get and insert into the .htaccess file that we talked about earlier.

Check Your Files

If the hack was directly against your WordPress site, you want to make sure you scan all of your files to ensure that there are no malicious programs hiding within them. Also scan your plugins, themes and other possible sources of entry.

Keep in mind that sometimes even the best virus and malware scanners can miss bits of malicious code that have been inserted into your files. This is especially true for your .htaccess file.

Check the .htaccess File

Make sure that your .htaccess file hasn't been compromised. Since this file is so important to security, you need to make sure that it hasn't been altered with malicious code. Make certain you scroll through the entire code; hackers like to hide their code in hard-to-notice locations.

To easily locate malicious code, compare your .htaccess file against a clean .htaccess file. (You can do this for any other files you check manually, too.)

A default .htaccess file will look like:

```
# BEGIN WordPress
<ifmodule mod_rewrite.c>
RewriteEngine On
RewriteBase /
RewriteCond %{REQUEST_FILENAME} !-f
RewriteCond %{REQUEST_FILENAME} !-d
RewriteRule . /index.php [L]
</ifmodule>
# END WordPress
```

or, in some cases, simply like this if it is a placeholder devoid of any real code:

```
# BEGIN WordPress

# END WordPress
```

Keep an eye out for strange code that you didn't add.

Also, keep in mind that a hacker may decide to change the access permissions on your .htaccess file or other important files on your server. Change them back to their original settings as soon as possible if they have been altered.

Malicious Code to Look Out For

Here are some bits of code that could signify a hacker:

```
eval ()

base64_decode ()

POST: Array
(
[cookie] => wordpressuser_c73ce9557defbe87cea780be67f9ae1f=xyz%27;
wordpresspass_c73ce9557defbe87cea780be67f9ae1f=132;
)

<?xml version="1.0"?>

<methodCall>

<methodName>test.method

</methodName>

<params>

<param>

<value><name>','')); echo

`_____BEGIN_____';

passthru('id');

echo

`_____FIM_____';

exit;/*</name></value>

</param>

</params>

</methodCall>
```

Malicious code like this could be in *any* .php file on your WordPress site. Since malicious code can be so hard to find, a complete deletion/uninstall of your site may be necessary.

Sometimes, malicious code will be sneaked in as an image and added to the activated plugins list. To see if this has happened, go into PHPMyAdmin, locate your site's options table, and then find the active_plugins record. Look for code that looks like this:

```
../uploads/2008/05/04/jhjyahjhnjnva.jpg
```

If you find this code, delete it. Note that there may be multiple instances of this code. If you are having a hard time tracking them all down, just delete your active_plugins record and reinstall all plugins.

Delete Everything (optional)

If the attack was directly against your website and not an intrusion into your computer, you may want to consider deleting your site in its entirety, since malicious code can be hard to find. This is why it is important to back up your files so that you can upload a clean copy of the site that is free of malicious code in this situation.

If you decide to do this, make sure that your backup files haven't been compromised as well. If the hacker got into your hosting server, there is a chance that he or she could have done something to your backup files too.

In some cases, you may even want to go so far as to completely remove the installation of WordPress from your server and do a fresh install. This will ensure that no malicious code remains in your files, as they will all have been completely deleted, even the folders themselves.

Back to Normal

If you do get hacked, use it as a learning experience. Figure out how the hacker got into your site and install security measures to make sure that it doesn't happen again. There is a chance that the hacker may try again, so it is very important that you defend against future attacks, especially those that use the original method to get into your system.

Chapter 6: DDoS and What to Do if You're Attacked

DDoS stands for Distributed Denial of Service. DDoS attacks are carried out by hackers using compromised computer systems that all target the same system. They flood the selected server with requests and force the system to go offline. Due to how easy it is to carry out a DDoS attack, they are fairly common.

You can think of your website as a room. Only so many people can stand inside this room at once, but that's okay, because you normally don't reach maximum capacity, anyway. However, if someone were to come by and fill your room with boxes, no one would be able to get inside.

This is similar to what a DDoS does. All of the controlled computers contact the website at the same time. The server responds to their requests, using up all of the system's resources. Because of this, legitimate users won't be able to access your website. It is difficult to track these attacks down, because the computers used for the crime could be in different locations all around the world.

If you think you might be targeted by a DDoS attack, try to confirm it. If you host your website on your own server, is your Internet connection slower than usual? The massive amounts of requests you'll be getting will slow your entire connection. If your website is remotely hosted, then does your site time out when you try to connect?

I'm Under Attack! What do I Do?

You need to be aware of your options when you create a defense plan. Ideally, you'll have a plan prepared before you get attacked, but sometimes things just don't work out that way. Unfortunately, just as extra security can cost a bit of money, so should you be prepared to spend a bit more to get your site back up.

Call in Some Help

If you're being DDoS attacked, you want to contact your ISP (if you host yourself) or your web host. You also want to call your security network. It could be that they already know; they're likely to have already noticed the spike in traffic.

Your web host will want to deal with this problem as quickly as you do, since the high requests can slow down multiple servers in their network. It's a good idea to contact them instead of just letting them handle the situation on their own, because their method of dealing with it may not be the one you want. For example, if you are being DDoS attacked, your web host may redirect your traffic to null. This basically means that all incoming traffic will be sent to a non-existent server, meaning no one will be able to connect to your website.

Ask your host if they offer alternate solutions. Some hosts will offer mitigation services for DDoS attacks, like firewalls and proxies. Firewalls, switches, proxies and scripts can help sort out fake requests and let the good ones through. These may be costly, however, and not all hosts will offer them.

Your network security will work with you and try to help you through your problem. (After all, that's why you pay them, right?) Your web host, on the other hand, may have specific policies regarding what to do in this situation. They are not guaranteed to act in your favor, and it's a good idea to read the policies on their site to see how they might react.

If the attacks are small, you may have the option to upgrade to a better hosting plan that would allow you to take the brunt of the attack and still let legitimate users through. This may be a good answer if you find you are consistently attacked; however, if you choose to take this course of action, your attacker may decide to step up their methods as well. Talk to your provider about your options.

If you run your own server, try installing firewalls. Configure these firewalls along with your switches, routers, etc. to sort out the spam and let the real people through to your website.

File a Police Report

DDoS attacks are illegal, and you should report the crime to your local authorities. This won't help you get your server back online, and you will probably never know if your report helps lead to any arrests. But giving the information to the police can help lead to solutions in the long run. If you call, be sure to dial their non-emergency number; don't tie up 911 or your local emergency number. Expect them to ask a lot of questions, because odds are they don't have a DDoS specialist on staff.

However, you may want to check your local disclosure laws before you report the attack. Once you tell the police, they may have the ability to tell whomever they want, and this could give your website negative attention. In rare instances, they may even confiscate your computer for investigation into the attacks.

Wait it out

Sometimes the simplest solutions are the best. (Well, maybe "best" isn't the right word.) If you've stepped up your security and upgraded your servers, and the attacks continue to take down your site, there isn't a whole lot you can do.

DDoS attacks are difficult to track down and stop, but they can't last forever. The longer a DDoS attack continues, the more the hacker risks being caught. It's also likely the hacker will get bored or lose interest. Sooner or later, they will stop.

There is no guarantee that, once the attack has stopped, that they won't try again. The more spam you can filter out through your firewalls and other security systems, the better. But if your methods aren't working, your only choice may be to wait

Chapter 7: Password Tricks

Having a strong password is one of the most fundamental ways to stop hacking attempts. The "brute force" method of hacking is when a hacker uses a program to try thousands, if not millions, of password combinations to get into your account. The secret key method discussed earlier, as well as other strategies and tricks, can help reduce the chance of a hacker getting into your website this way.

Creating a Strong Password

The first step to password protection is to create a very strong password. Passwords that use all numbers, all letters, or a simple combination of the two aren't as strong as you'd think. To get around this problem, here are some basic tips for creating a strong password.

- Make sure it is more than eight characters long.

- If you can, include numbers, symbols, and a combination of uppercase and lowercase letters

- Avoid guessable passwords, such as dictionary words, names of family or loved ones and birth dates.

Another thing you want to do is visit a site that will gauge the strength of your password. You can use a pretty good one by using this website `http://www.passwordmeter.com/`.

These passwords can be very hard to remember, so it is recommended that you either physically write down your passwords and store them in a very secure location or take the time to thoroughly memorize them. Memorization can be helped by saying the password out loud on a regular basis or by associating mental images with the password using mnemonic memory techniques.

You can also go to `http://www.wikihow.com/Create-a-Password-You-Can-Remember` for some tips on how to create an easy to remember password, but be aware that some of the tips in this resource do not focus on creating a strong security password.

Change your Password Regularly

Another thing you should be doing is changing your WordPress passwords regularly. You can do this once a month, or even once a week if you want to be really secure. This will ensure that hackers don't have an easy time accessing your site.

Also, make sure that, in the event that you need to allow a web designer, security systems expert or anyone else to modify your site, that you delete their user accounts when they're done. If they will be working with you on an ongoing basis, ensure that you also change their password regularly as well.

The Static/Variable Method

Since changing your password regularly can strain your brain in a major way when it comes to recall, you can use this little trick. Have one half of your password be very hard to guess and always remain the same. The second half will be an easy-to-remember phrase or word that you can swap out at regular intervals with other easy-to-remember word combinations.

Here are a few examples:

- G8)?gR02ndogfood

- uq!8P29L*beartrap

- aR'_e+89K^gonefishing

Concentrate on memorizing the hard part. You'll only need to do that once, and then swap out the easy-to-remember part as needed.

Alternate Key Strokes

Another clever way to create a password is simply to change the position of your hands on the keyboard. While this doesn't make use of special symbols, it can be handy in cases where you aren't allowed to create a password using those symbols.

For example, if you move your fingers one key to the right from the default position, "dogfood" becomes "fphgppf." Used creatively, you can easily remember your password using this technique while throwing off hackers who look for common words at the same time.

Password Protected Pages

Also, remember that you can also password-protect specific pages on your website. If you are doing this, you need to ensure that there is no intrusion into these areas. To help facilitate this, use a different password than the one you use to log into your admin account. This can confuse hackers and make it hard for them to access multiple private areas.

Another great thing about this is the fact that multiple password layers buy you time in the event of a hack — the extra time may be enough to take care of the hacker problem before they get into all of your data.

The #1 Rule

The most important thing to remember about your WordPress passwords is to make sure that they are not the same as any other passwords you use online. Your admin area, cPanel, webpages and anything else passworded should each have its own unique password. If you use the same password for everything, a hacker's job is much easier and they can get into all of your data in one fell swoop.

Conclusion

Keeping your WordPress site secure does take some time and effort. There are a variety of threats out there that you'll need to prepare for. Learning what steps you can take is just the first part; now you'll need to put them into action.

The Internet is always changing and hackers will keep trying to come up with new ways to get into your system. You'll need to stay on your toes and keep one step ahead of them. There are plenty of tools and tricks you can use that will keep you in the game.

There are all sorts of plugins and software programs that you can use to keep unwanted intruders at bay. Avoid simple mistakes that leave you exposed, such as password sharing and using public computers. Stay updated on all of your programs and plugins. Also, keep your files backed up, so if the worst happens, you still have all of your data saved. Having strong passwords can keep hackers from ever getting in.

Getting hacked isn't the end of the world. It can be quite the thorn in your side, but you always have options available to you. Your security network and web host can help you regain control of your site, while security software can help you clean up your system and prevent future attacks.

Losing control of your website can be unsettling, and it may take some time to clean up, but there's no such thing as an adversity that you can't learn from. Hackers are out to ruin the Internet for the rest of us, either for their own enjoyment or for some sort of gain. However, there are tons of ways to protect yourself and keep using the largest network in the world.

Your Friend,

Lambert

Resources

Anti-virus for Windows

avast! Antivirus

`http://www.avast.com/`

AVG Internet Security

`http://www.avg.com/`

Avira Antivirus Premium

`http://www.avira.com/en/for-home-avira-antivirus-premium-v1`

McAfee AntiVirus Plus

`http://home.mcafee.com/store/antivirus-plus`

Norton AntiVirus

`http://us.norton.com/antivirus/`

ZoneAlarm Antivirus + Firewall

`http://www.zonealarm.com/security/en-us/zonealarm-antivirus-software.htm`

Anti-virus for Mac

Avira Free Mac Security

`http://www.avira.com/en/download-start/product/avira-free-mac-security`

McAfee VirusScan for Mac

`http://www.mcafee.com/us/products/virusscan-for-mac.aspx`

Norton Antivirus for Mac

`http://us.norton.com/macintosh-antivirus/`

Misc. Free Protection

Comodo Firewall for Windows

`http://personalfirewall.comodo.com/`

ZoneAlarm Free Firewall by Checkpoint

`http://www.zonealarm.com/security/en/trialpay-za-signup.htm`

Misc. Paid Protection

Comodo Antivirus and Firewall

`http://personalfirewall.comodo.com/`

Sandboxie

`http://sandboxie.com/`

ZoneAlarm PRO Firewall
http://www.zonealarm.com/security/en-us/zonealarm-pro-firewall-anti-spyware.htm

Cloud Storage Companies

JustCloud
http://www.justcloud.com/

SkyDrive
http://windows.microsoft.com/en-US/skydrive/home

ZipCloud
http://www.zipcloud.com/

Livedrive
http://www.livedrive.com/

SOS Online Backup
http://www.sosonlinebackup.com/

SugarSync
https://www.sugarsync.com/

Mozy
http://mozy.com/

Amazon S3
http://aws.amazon.com/s3/

DropBox
https://www.dropbox.com/

External Hard Drives

Seagate FreeAgent GoFlex Drives
http://www.seagate.com/www/en-us/products/external/external-hard-drive/

Seagate Expansion Hard Drives
http://www.seagate.com/www/en-us/products/external/expansion/

Western Digital External Desktop Hard Drives
http://www.wdc.com/en/products/external/desktop/

LaCie Desktop Hard Drives
http://www.lacie.com/products/range.htm?id=10033

SQL Tutorial

Bluehost: MySQL Database Creation
https://my.bluehost.com/cgi/help/6

Host Gator: How do I create a MySQL database, a user, and then delete if needed?

`http://support.hostgator.com/articles/cpanel/how-do-i-create-a-mysql-database-a-user-and-then-delete-if-needed`

Security Plugins

Login and Admin

Semisecure Login Reimagined

`http://wordpress.org/extend/plugins/semisecure-login-reimagined/`

Login LockDown

`http://wordpress.org/extend/plugins/login-lockdown/`

Chap Secure Login

`http://wordpress.org/extend/plugins/chap-secure-login/`

Admin SSL
`http://wordpress.org/extend/plugins/admin-ssl-secure-admin/`

Backup

WP-DB-Backup

`http://wordpress.org/extend/plugins/wp-db-backup/`

Remote Database Backup

`http://wordpress.org/extend/plugins/remote-database-backup/`

WP-DBManager

`http://wordpress.org/extend/plugins/wp-dbmanager/`

BackUpWordPress

`http://wordpress.org/extend/plugins/backupwordpress/`

myEASYbackup

`http://myeasywp.com/plugins/myeasybackup/`

Spam Block

Antispam Bee

`http://wordpress.org/extend/plugins/antispam-bee/`

NoSpamNX

`http://wordpress.org/extend/plugins/nospamnx/`

Aksimet
`http://akismet.com/`

Defensio Anti-Spam

`http://wordpress.org/extend/plugins/defensio-anti-spam/`

SI CAPTCHA Anti-Spam

`http://wordpress.org/extend/plugins/si-captcha-for-wordpress/`

WP-reCAPTCHA

`http://wordpress.org/extend/plugins/wp-recaptcha/`

Blackhole

`http://perishablepress.com/blackhole-bad-bots/`

Security

Secure WordPress

`http://wordpress.org/extend/plugins/secure-wordpress/`

WP Security Scan

`http://wordpress.org/extend/plugins/wp-security-scan/`

AskApache Password Protect

`http://wordpress.org/extend/plugins/askapache-password-protect/`

TAC (Theme Authenticity Checker)

`http://wordpress.org/extend/plugins/tac/`

HTTP Authentication

`http://wordpress.org/extend/plugins/http-authentication/`

AntiVirus

`http://wordpress.org/extend/plugins/antivirus/`

Replace WP-Version

`http://wordpress.org/extend/plugins/replace-wp-version/`

WP Email Guard

`http://wordpress.org/extend/plugins/wp-email-guard/`

WordPress File Monitor

`http://wordpress.org/extend/plugins/wordpress-file-monitor/`

wp-dephorm

`http://wordpress.org/extend/plugins/wp-dephorm/`

WordPress Firewall

`http://wordpress.org/extend/plugins/wordpress-firewall/`

Secure Contact

`http://wordpress.org/extend/plugins/secure-contact-form/`

Fast Secure Contact Form

`http://wordpress.org/extend/plugins/si-contact-form/`

Content Security Policy

`http://wordpress.org/extend/plugins/content-security-policy/`

FTP Programs

Cyberduck

`http://cyberduck.ch/`

FileZilla

`http://filezilla-project.org/`

JSCAPE

`http://www.jscape.com/`

WinSCP

`http://winscp.net/eng/index.php`

RAID Setup Tutorial

Windows

How to set up a RAID array on your motherboard

`http://www.youtube.com/watch?v=rgo0OPSw9_E`

RAID 0 & RAID 1 Setup Guide (NCIX Tech Tips #77)

`http://www.youtube.com/watch?v=RYBtmVMtH1g`

RAID 5 & RAID 10 Tutorial & Explanation (NCIX Tech Tips #79)

`http://www.youtube.com/watch?v=TuwjadbtUCY`

Mac

How to set up RAID on a Mac 2012

`http://www.youtube.com/watch?v=NbG1G3sNqwk`

Mac Pro RAID installation

`http://www.youtube.com/watch?v=U41beKVajao`

External Hard Drive Setup

How to Set Up and Connect an External Hard Drive to your Mac

`http://www.youtube.com/watch?v=ocKvU9yzPAc`

Western Digital 750GB External Hard Drive

`http://www.youtube.com/watch?v=-xok11PpjAE`

Network Attached Storage Devices

A short cartoon explaining what a NAS can do for your home network

`http://www.youtube.com/watch?v=-1L_2G6rLI0`

Western Digital Network Products

http://www.wdc.com/en/products/network/

Buffalo Tech - NAS Product Selector

http://www.buffalotech.com/products/network-storage/product-selector/

Security Firms

eSoft

http://www.esoft.com/network-security-solutions/web-security-solution/

Miles Consulting

http://www.milesconsultingcorp.com/IT-Outsourcing.aspx

SecureWorks

http://www.secureworks.com/

Trustwave

https://www.trustwave.com/encryption/

Places to Hire Freelance Security Help

Freelanced Social Network

http://www.freelanced.com/jobs/network-security/us

Freelancer

http://www.freelancer.com/jobs/Computer-Security/

Guru

http://www.guru.com/

Secret Key Generator

Secret Key Generator

https://api.wordpress.org/secret-key/1.1/salt/

Related Products

WordPress Domination: Beginner to Ninja in 7 Days

```
http://www.amazon.com/WordPress-Domination-Beginner-NINJA-
ebook/dp/B007LS0TLE/
```

How to Get Free Traffic: Free Unique Ways to Send Visitors to your Websites & Blogs

```
http://www.amazon.com/How-Get-Free-Traffic-ebook/dp/B004GEAGUA/
```

The Ultimate WordPress Themes and Plugins Review Guide

http://www.amazon.com/dp/B00B35YH4G

About the Author

Lambert Klein is that inspirational older brother you wish you had—that guy who knows all the ways to be successful at online marketing and is willing to share his secrets with you.

After leaving his job in construction, Lambert was determined to learn about Internet marketing. He successfully reinvented himself as an authentic and dedicated writer focusing on Internet solutions and Internet marketing. He started out writing for other people, and soon realized that he could work on his own projects exclusively and produce a generous income.

His uncompromising passion to write quality content has driven his four websites to wild success. He found that the people around him were constantly coming to him for advice on Internet marketing. That was the moment he knew that he would begin writing books about Internet solutions.

Lambert has authored several PDF reports and e-books, as well as a variety of Kindle books, covering such subjects as blogging, search engine optimization, weight loss, and natural anti-aging. He's most proud of the response to his most popular book on Amazon Kindle, entitled *WordPress Power Guide*.

Lambert calls Marion Township home, where he lives on seven acres of beautiful Michigan countryside. There, you will find him hiking with his wife Lynn or strumming on his guitar. On the weekends, he enjoys heading to the ballpark to take in a Detroit Tigers baseball game, playing with his cat Mitts, or enjoying a double scoop of chocolate ice cream.

It's said that you should find someone whom you want to be like and copy them. Lambert Klein is that guy. He knows Internet marketing, he's making money, and he's willing to share his knowledge with you.

Contact Information: http://www.lambertklein.com/

Lambert Klein

www.ingramcontent.com/pod-product-compliance
Lightning Source LLC
Chambersburg PA
CBHW060500060326
40689CB00020B/4600